THE MIDDLE MAN
How to be successful as a young man

Stephen Swinson

Copyright © 2015 by Stephen Swinson

The Middle Man
How to be successful as a young man
by Stephen Swinson

Printed in the United States of America.

ISBN 9781498449328

All rights reserved solely by the author. The author guarantees all contents are original and do not infringe upon the legal rights of any other person or work. No part of this book may be reproduced in any form without the permission of the author. The views expressed in this book are not necessarily those of the publisher.

Unless otherwise indicated, Scripture quotations are taken from the New King James Version (NKJV). Copyright © 1979, 1980, 1982 by Thomas Nelson, Inc. Used by permission. All rights reserved.

www.xulonpress.com

TABLE OF CONTENTS

Introduction..vii

Chapter 1: LAG Principle 9
Chapter 2: Know your gift, hone your skills
and always be prepared for an opportunity... 13
Chapter 3: The Character, Integrity and the
Spiritual Resume of Joseph 17
Chapter 4: What can I do to help myself?
Build your faith; don't be discouraged......21
Chapter 5: Meditating on God's word day
and night is the key to our success. 25

Conclusion 31
Pray with me 33

Introduction

All men are determined to find their own unique way towards a successful life. Wherever it is, we want to get there; by any means necessary. Yet, how many of us find ourselves stuck in the middle phase of life? Where everything doesn't make sense and where we are trying to find ourselves. Where we are still trying to become a man and be viewed as such within our society. Where we want to do something meaningful and not just monotonous. This "middle phase" can leave us worse for the wear, as we realize that we have gained absolutely nothing through the phase itself. If you were to ask another man that is doing well, "How did you get to where you are today?" and "Do you have any advice?", You can expect to get responses that range from "I worked my entire life to get where I am, you should do that" to, "I was in the Army, Marines or the Navy, you should try that". To some of us, that response just isn't good enough. That brings me to the purpose of writing this book. God has instilled something special in every man; to have empathy, to love, to nurture, to protect and to lead. However, leading spiritually can be a big issue. Especially, in the moments when we feel like God has forgotten about us, and that we're on a path that is going nowhere fast, it is so easy to develop a disconnect between us and God. Still, we never really take time to address the lack of connection, so we develop into grown men that haven't matured in this area. As a result we have nothing to give to the future young men coming behind us, nor our girlfriends, fiancés or spouses. How can we fix that disconnect? How can we go in the direction that God has mapped out for us? How can we become fulfilled? How can we become the man that God has created us to be? I answer all of those questions in the following pages of this book. God has helped me to understand the key to having a fulfilled life and getting out of the "black hole" phase that most men experience Some of us have life handed to us, while others receive nothing for free—no guidance, no direction and no career. Well, for the men that need the keys to success in their life, HERE IT IS! Pay close attention and take notes!

Chapter 1
LAG PRINCIPLE

When you are in that middle phase of life, you need to make sure that you are constantly exerting your energy in an area. For example, let's say you have a degree, but you are not hired, not doing what you want to do in life, and not exactly sure what it is that God has created you to do. Solution: FIND SOMETHING TO DO! You, as a man, have to keep yourself busy! Learn a new language, make or create something. Personally, I have been able to keep myself busy by: creating and then following a specific resistance training program, mastering a mixing software and producing software, creating my own genre of music (the relatively untapped market of Christian electro house music), cutting men's hair, training football players for speed, and now, publishing a book. I will be the most eloquent and well-rounded man, whether I have a job, a degree or not! I have to remind myself of that every day.

It is very easy to sit back and sulk until someone hands something to you that makes you a man. Let me explain. When we are unemployed (or simply waiting to figure out something we're good at), we begin to think that a job will either give us the money we need to feel like a man, or that a title will prove that our time is valuable, so we won't feel worthless. I can date someone, pick up the tab every time we go out to eat, pay my bills, and put gas in my car. But to the theory that a job will give you the worth you're looking for and the purpose for your life, I give a big resounding NO! Don't wait for tangible things to make you feel like, look like, or act like a man. MAKE YOURSELF A MAN! Learn, adapt, grow! This is what I call the "LAG Principle".

You can apply the LAG principle to your life at any time, but specifically when your life seems to be lacking direction, moving slowly, or not in the direction that you feel you have control over it, LAG!

- Learn- Understand the details of what is going on in your specific situation.

- Adapt- Become flexible enough to deal with the situation until you can change it, and most importantly.
- Grow- (Most important) Apply your new understanding and flexibility to other situations.

If you apply these steps whenever you find yourself in a tough situation, you will ultimately master the LAG Principle. This is the key!

God created Adam, in Genesis, and gave him dominion over all things. In contrast, to Adam we go about life following others, wallowing in our shortcomings, feeling sad about our disappointments and becoming depressed by life itself. This is NOT what we are called to do. We must lead, we must conquer our lives and have dominion. Now, it might be helpful to look at a real-life success story for inspiration, as we attempt to transform ourselves to live according to our calling. The greatest example of all is the character that will be the headline of this entire book, a man named Joseph. Stay with me, as I outline his entire life and we work together to guide you out of your phase in life known as "the middle man."

—As a man, most people don't validate this stage of life for us. They don't tell us they understand, or "I'll help you". Instead, they simply use us as an example of what not to be- "Don't be a slob like your brother." The impact of friends, loved ones and society haphazardly spewing powerful, but demeaning, comments of that nature does nothing but crush many of us as men. It becomes so easy to feel worthless and like your life is unnecessary. If you ever find yourself in this stage of life, there is hope! The second that you begin to feel as though life is unbearable, you can think of the life of Joseph, and your outlook on things may change.

Chapter 2

KNOW YOUR GIFT, HONE YOUR SKILLS AND ALWAYS BE PREPARED FOR AN OPPORTUNITY.

Joseph started off as a dreamer, knowing his gift. Although the people around him were jealous and aimed to crush him, he never lost heart and gave up. In response, God rewarded him for being faithful. (Now if you're that little brother telling your family your dreams, that you will rule over them and that they will bow to you, then this same thing might happen to you. Just a heads up.) We need to follow Joseph's example; Live with purpose and be faithful. Be a good steward of the gifts God has given you. There may not be a clear cut structure as to what you should be doing, but you should always have a plan, and you should attack the plan wholeheartedly each time. Remember: If you fail, continue to seek God for His purpose. (Proverbs 19:21) But if you succeed, you succeed! Go be effective! You don't need any counsel on that! Now, In the meantime, in between time; Get up in the morning! Shower! Read! Do something! The second you allow yourself to accept laziness (whenever you allow yourself to not have a healthy routine) you begin to lose some of what makes you feel like a man. Have a routine. Prepare yourself for that job that you're waiting for. Get up, shower, read, work on an idea or invention, go work out, drink water, get adequate sleep.

Treat this period in the same manner you would as you prepare for a visit to the dentist's office. As I explain what I mean by this, keep an image of a " waiting room" in mind. For weeks and months you have brushed your teeth, flossed and used mouthwash. These behaviors could be easily described by e terms like "routine," and "consistency", right? Ok, stay with me. The night before your upcoming dentist's appointment, you continue to do what you've been doing *consistently* for all this time, rather than something you are just for the first time really on the night before (although if we're honest, this is sometimes the case). The actual day of the appointment, you also brush your teeth and use that same routine. You drive to the dentist's office, you park and you walk in. You put your name on the list or you tell the receptionist that you are here for your appointment. Now, you are in the waiting room. Have you done what was necessary to prepare up until this point? Are you confident that you put in the necessary work, time and energy? Are you prepared to go in and show your teeth off? Hopefully, you are able to respond "yes"; but sometimes, in our lives as men, we are not. We are not ready when opportunities present themselves, and of course that is a bad reflection on us. Out of that lack of preparation usually comes a "no." But that "no" that we may hear may spiral us back into the conundrum that we were just in, and unnecessarily. In order to prevent this, you have to be prepared. How can you prepare yourself for something that you might not know anything about? When there's nothing but a question mark in your brain about what you should know or what to expect, I can tell you that sitting around, feeling sorry for yourself (and current state) and doing nothing are the wrong answers.

Chapter 3

THE CHARACTER, INTEGRITY AND THE SPIRITUAL RESUME OF JOSEPH

(Joseph Chapters 37 to 41)

Joseph was sold into slavery as a young man; but he ultimately became second in command, only to Pharaoh. How did he do that? Not by hustling hard and asking God to bless it. Joseph made this accomplishment by knowing his gift (and how to use it), being positive in every position he was in, keeping busy, trusting God, and having character plus integrity. His gift did indeed make room for him. Joseph knew that he had the gift of dreams, and there interpretations. Because of it, he made his way out of the jail. A butler of the pharaoh simply remembered there was a man, (Joseph) who interpreted his dream at one point, while he himself was in jail. Joseph always trusted God and never lost sight of his gifts. He was positive about the position he was in. It is very common to complain and mope around about the things that are happening in our lives. But during our "middle man" period we must remember that God is still God; His ways are higher than our ways; His thoughts are higher than our thoughts (Isaiah 55:8-9) and that He has thoughts that are good towards us, to prosper us and give us a hope (Jeremiah 29:11). Joseph kept busy by working in the Pharaoh's house and by being keeper of the jail. Joseph was always doing something! It never says anywhere in the word that he was lying around or idle; he was doing something or in charge of something. When Joseph was given the keys to the jail, he didn't say, "No thank you, I'm good. I've never done this before." or, "No thanks, I'm depressed; I'm nobody". This man, even in the face of utter hopelessness, was in charge and doing something! How many of us will wallow, and allow sadness and depression to set in at that point? How many of us will say, "Well this is not what I want to do, it's not a goal of mine". Joseph took what he could get and mastered it. That looks great on a physical resume. Finally, Joseph had character. Integrity is what you do when nobody's looking; when no one can see your decisions but you and God. Character is who you are when you can't help it. What you practice (integrity), is what will come out effortlessly. Pharaoh's wife tried to sleep with Joseph! And guess what Joseph did when she made advances? He ran! How many of us would have stayed and heard some nice things about ourselves? How good we look, how handsome we are? We would have flirted with that thing and gotten caught up! If Joseph would've stayed and taken what was given to him he would've been washing windows in Pharaoh's house for the rest of his life, or worse! He would've been killed if the Pharaoh would have ever caught wind of an affair! Thank God, for our sakes, that Joseph ran. And thank God, for Joseph's sake, that he ran. Joseph needed to be led and pointed in the right direction, and he was! His integrity was what led him; not necessarily having favor with all the right people, knowing the right guys, or being cool. The ability to make the right decisions in the dark (when nobody was watching); that's what led him! "The integrity of the righteous shall lead them" (Proverbs 11:3).

In your own personal dark period, allow God to work on the areas in your life that still need work. For Joseph, his area was forgiveness. After everything that had been done to him in life, he still had it in his heart to bless his family. Joseph had the power to lock them all away in jail, or kill them, but he didn't. What a testimony to God's work on his character.

Chapter 4

WHAT CAN I DO TO HELP MYSELF? BUILD YOUR FAITH; DON'T BE DISCOURAGED.

(Matthew 25:14-30), (Romans 10:17)

Listen guys; You must have faith in this valley of life you're in. Don't be depressed, you must have faith! Without faith it is impossible to please God! In other words, you will never get out of your present situation, or see any hope in it, without having faith. Hebrews eleven six says that without faith it is impossible to please God. If you continue reading, the Bible also says that "anyone who comes to Him must believe that He exists and that He rewards those who earnestly seek Him". God rewards those that believe; those that fight through the depression and fight through the bleakness of their situation. In the book of Joshua (chapter one verse nine), God gives a simple command. The verse says "Have I not commanded you? Be strong and very courageous [...] for the Lord thy God is with you". I consider being a pushover in this area, and being defeated, disobedient to God's command. In the parable of the Talents (Matthew 25:14-30), three men are given talents; one was given five, one given two, one man given one. The servant with five talents went and traded for five more, the man with two talents also doubled his, and the man with one buried his in the ground. "I only got one", "This isn't enough money to even do anything with", "You might as well take your money back" are all statements that represent this unjust stewards' attitude. Yet, we communicate this same language to God when we sit back lazily with the literal talents that He's given us. No matter how many He gives us, we as men, had better fight to the death, to maximize the potential God has given us. At the end of the parable it says that each man had to give an account for the money that they were each given. The men that received the five talents and two talents were commended for getting a return on His original investment. However, the conversation, between the master and the third man (who had one talent and buried it in the ground), began with "You wicked and lazy servant!" He ended by saying in descriptive detail, "For to everyone who has, more will be given, and he will have abundance; but from him who does not have, even what he has will be taken away. And cast the unprofitable servant into the outer darkness. There will be weeping and gnashing of teeth." Do not, I repeat do not be the wicked and lazy servant; do what God has commanded you to do. Now that that's clear; how do we build our faith? Simple; we build our faith by hearing, and hearing the word of God (Romans 10:17). Hear the word! Listen to sermons and podcasts of your favorite pastors over and over. Get that word down in your spirit until you can regurgitate it.

Chapter 5

MEDITATING ON GOD'S WORD DAY AND NIGHT IS THE KEY TO OUR SUCCESS.

(Joshua 1:8, 2 Timothy 1:7, 101:3-4, Matthew 4:4, Ephesians 6:13, Proverbs 14:16, Proverbs 8:13)

Let me tell you the secret to your success. Write this down, put it as an alert on your smartphone, stick it to your bedroom wall or your bathroom mirror. The key is, "BIBLICAL MEDITATION". And yes, that is in all caps. Do NOT forget that.

Joshua 1:8 says "This book of the law shall not depart from your mouth, but you shall meditate in it day and night that you may observe to do according to all that is written in it. For then you will make your way prosperous then you will have good success". Notice the placement of "then". The success is contingent on something! Wow! Mind blowing right? Didn't know it was that simple? Well, God made it very clear. For some reason it is a principal we will overlook in a heartbeat. We will go out and read the story of Steve Jobs and be inspired for some reason about what he did to get where he got. But we have it all wrong. You dare look at one of God's creations to figure out a plan for which to base your life, rather than looking towards the actual creator? We compare ourselves to other people, then try to figure out why the plan that *they* followed doesn't yield similar results when we do the same in *our* life. I am so guilty of doing it myself. We do it all the time. It should sound ludicrous, but it goes as an unchecked thought. Remember: Absorb a successful man's habits, but primarily focus on God's word. Seek God's special purpose for your life. It's a genius strategy really. Meditate on God's word day and night, *then* the success that He guarantees in your life will come. God IS; He hasn't stopped existing. He created the universe, the heavens, the earth, and God created YOU. Follow the creator of the universe, trust me; this is your only hope.

Finally, there's another major benefit to meditating on the word of God. Not only will you be successful, but the word of God will be down on the inside of you! You'd be surprised by how important that is. This is the key to living a life that's not just successful, but also free. Imagine being tempted to watch porn, engage in sex and give into lust but the word of God rises up and you regurgitate the appropriate scripture at the appropriate time. Trust me, it's a struggle to spend so much time dwelling on the word, but do you not understand that you are engaging in spiritual warfare. How do you fight back? With the word of God of course! Satan tempted Jesus when He had fasted forty days and forty nights. In Matthew 4:4 Jesus said, "It is written, 'Man shall not live by bread alone, but by every word that proceeds from the mouth of God." Secondly, "It is written again, you shall not tempt the Lord your God". Jesus quoted the word of God! He fought back! He didn't simply use willpower. He regurgitated the appropriate scripture at the right time. How key this is for us as men; fighting back using the sword of the spirit, which is the word of God! We can be easily defeated in a physical fight if we never fight back. Not only is throwing a punch a great idea, but hitting your enemy would be even better! That's being effective! Take the compelling grip of fear and the giant gorilla that jumps on your back called lust, for example. A lot of men deal with these two things, but don't share. How do you take up your sword in these two areas? First, with fear, (false evidence appearing real) 2 Timothy 1:7 gives us a clear direction to wield our sword; "For God has not given us a spirit of fear, but of power and of love and of a sound mind". God did not even give us the spirit of fear! Why do we let it seize and run our lives? We have been equipped by God with a strong mind and power! Those words strong and power mean we have the ability to conquer our circumstances that fear arises; remember that. Now, onto lust. When we're tempted by sex and pornography, this is the direction you wield your sword. Psalms 101:3-4 says "I will set nothing wicked before my eyes; I hate the work of those who fall away; It shall not cling to me. A perverse heart shall depart from me; I will not know wickedness." These two verses are so powerful. Get this in your heart; I WILL NOT set anything wicked before my eyes, and not only that but I hate the work of those who fall away. Let me pause and deal with that part. *I hate the work of those who fall away.* This means "Anyone who isn't chasing God like I am, isn't giving their life over to God every single day, and their relationship with God isn't reflecting in their work, then their work isn't worth me defiling myself and feeding myself with." That point should be huge for every man reading this book. Porn is the work of those who have fallen away. Music that is explicit and raunchy, television and movies that are provocative, are examples of the work of those who have fallen away. I'm not saying never watch another movie or television show, but I am saying ask yourself this: *Do I hate the work of those who have fallen away? Or do I secretly like their work and look forward to it every week?*

The next part of the passage is *a perverse heart shall depart from me, I will not know wickedness.* What a big deal this is. You say a command to yourself that a wicked heart shall depart from you. If we're all honest we do like things that cause us to lust and regress in our renewed minds, at times. But repeat this part of the verse and say "In the name of Jesus, a wicked heart will depart from me." God gives us a sword for a reason. The Word is a two-edged sword that cuts going in and coming out. It is not a spear or a crossbow. The Word is for up close and personal attacks; and you have the power to fight your enemy with nothing but confidence. Remember; the last part of the verse says, *I will not know wickedness.* That is so confident; let that mindset rub off on you when facing daily temptation. Even when you've done all you could to stand, all day, through work, through school, and through life's obstacles, stand some more. (Ephesians 6:13)

In order to be successful and defeat your enemy the devil day in and day out, not only must you hate him (The fear of God is to hate evil, *Proverbs 8:13*), but you must hide God's word in your heart, then you won't just sin against Him so readily (proverbs 14:16). Sin will no longer be your first reflex or instinctive. We are prepared now with the word of God!

Conclusion

If you feel you are in this "middle man" period of life, consider it the molding process. You could be just getting out of jail and can't find a job; apply this to your life. You could be taking a year before attending college or taking time off after attending college; you could be a high school athlete, college athlete, a high school student, a college student or even a grown man, currently in a relationship, engaged or married. Don't be too proud to read this information because it can apply to you wherever you are in life. God has blessed me with this information to give to you. Allow the words on the pages to jump out to you; pray and ask God to make you receptive to what you are reading, and give you "the ability to apply the information" (that's the definition of wisdom!). Do you really want to be successful? If so, apply this information to your life thoroughly. Commit to swelling in the presence of God and in the word of God; fall in love with God everyday.

Remember Joshua 1:8, meditate in God's word day AND night, then you will begin to do all things that are written in the word, and then you will make your way prosperous, AND THEN YOU WILL HAVE GOOD SUCCESS.

PRAY WITH ME:

Dear Heavenly Gracious Father, God who created all things, God who created all men. Thank you that you see us as your children, heirs to your throne, and as appointed authority and leaders; not as a servant and slaves. You see us as rulers and you've given us dominion of the earth. Please God, give us the strength to do the things you've called us to do. Give us the patience to wait on you and to be of a good courage. Thank you for strengthening our hearts. God thank you for your lovingkindness and tender mercy that doesn't fail. Thank you for pulling out of us talents and stirring up the gifts you've put in us. Thank for allowing us to be privy to this information, to a thriving relationship with you and the undeniable keys to success. Thank you for these practical principles and the ability to apply them. Please help us to do the little things, like hiding your word in our hearts, having faith and not giving into depression, paying our tithes, and being in love with you. We love you and we thank you for all these things in Jesus name we pray and give thanks, Amen.

www.ingramcontent.com/pod-product-compliance
Lightning Source LLC
LaVergne TN
LVHW021745060526
838200LV00052B/3477